FINISHING LINE PRESS

www.finishinglinepress.com

Songs of Deliverance

poems by

Susan Doble Kaluza

Finishing Line Press
Georgetown, Kentucky

Songs of Deliverance

ACKNOWLEDGMENTS

Grateful Acknowledgment is made to the following print journals for first
publishing some of the poems in this book.

Lost River Review: "Cannon Beach" and "Request"
Tammy Journal: "Dismantling the Tree"

And a special thank you to Concrete Wolf Press. "Songs of Deliverance" was
awarded a Finalist position in The 2017 Concrete Wolf Poetry Chapbook
Award contest.

Publisher: Leah Maines
Editor: Christen Kincaid
Cover Art: CC0 Public Domain
Author Photo: Susan Doble Kaluza
Cover Design: Elizabeth Maines McCleavy

Printed in the USA on acid-free paper.
Order online: www.finishinglinepress.com
also available on amazon.com

Author inquiries and mail orders:
Finishing Line Press
P. O. Box 1626
Georgetown, Kentucky 40324
U. S. A.

Table of Contents

*In memory
of my brother, Jay,
whose head on flight
into the storm
of colorectal cancer
ended quietly December 9, 2016.
This book is for him.*

i. Songs of Deliverance

Acceptance

"The gulf between absence and presence
is tiny, profound. I spent decades inching over
it, clinging to your hand…"

—Charles Atkinson

Postcards from the End

This morning leaning over the coffee pot,
I thought how great it would be to see you,
how fun to talk with you again in a large
kitchen, no laptops or curtains, like
on a farm near Lake Ontario. How
lyrical is the sound of *Lake Ontario*;
if you say it slowly it lifts you,
thin boned and sand-like, riffling
over bluffs toward the voice of Neil
Young, his guitar the alarm call
of killdeer *flying away without you;*
how distant and sad he sounded
even then, when you were strong,

firm footed and square
shouldered like a musk ox
on the ground; the phone rings
but it's a number
I don't recognize; I don't answer it,
but if I did I'd say don't bother me,
I'm waiting for the dead,

for the struck match-tips of dawn,
the dancing debuts of tree moss,
rock doves on the wing, house
sparrows, mute swans; I'm ready
to leave from anywhere to join you
in the upkeep of our wishes, for a long
life and uncomplicated days. I'm not
there now, but I'm heading to Pacific
City, horses on the beach, a week
with friends I've not yet informed.

Ode to the Loons

I don't know why God
is like a birdwatcher
and why with his gold
dipped binoculars,

spotted you on the
ground like a wing shot
pheasant or else a Kestrel
caught in a net; but he

called your name
and up you stepped
no questions asked or maybe
you did but no one

in the hospital room that day
could understand a damned
word you said, if you were talking
to them or some God knows

what; but I'm not worthy of these days
following your death, and spend much
time either looking for things
or tracking my losses

from the last millennium, like how
it's taken years to get to the bottom
of the pile of papers and files in just
one corner of my office; how every other

room in the house is a glass-like lake
of loons wailing the names of
my children asking where you've gone:
I am here. I am here. I am here

the loons call back for each one
absent in the now quiet evening
where the neighbors fall into
their usual rituals of calling dogs

and slamming doors and all
the while I'm trapped
in the undertow of these belongings,
uncapped words, scraps of paper

bearing quotes by William Stafford,
John Haines, Rodney Jones;
but it's Levine I miss the most,
his *names of the lost,* and yes

I know it's random
in the middle of this glass
lake so empty of the voices
of the un-called, the uncelebrated,

the ones left out in the cold on nights
the neighbors stoke their fireplace
and drink dry wine and laugh
like the world were theirs alone.

Dismantling the Tree

Three pieces. I dislodge
the top first, compress
the branches as they resist,
spring back like

opened clams against
my palms; even fake
and stripped of the
decorative trappings,

these limbs know the law
of gravity and how the equal
and opposite reaction to
everything that happens

in the universe is inexplicable,
is really a kind of curse
that goes unbroken even
as I reach the bottom and

re-arrange the stand's
disjointed legs to fit the box.
Brother, I thought of you
in the glare of those first

hypnotic bulbs, the season's
initial triumph against
shortened days, that sudden
cold snap swinging off

the frivolity of lights
strung across the deck.
You were the last
man I remember

could fix a frozen
pipe without complaining,
crush a Pabst Blue Ribbon can
between hand and wrist.

How was it your cells
spin doctoring multiples
of themselves
to keep from dying

could not save you
in your complexity,
not in the pieces that
were made of you

strapped against the chemo
pump, the plastic tubes
of junk they flooded
your bloodstream with.

Some tree you were,
you towering metaphor,
sprawling larch of human strength
impossible to duplicate

amid the fakery, the far flung,
like this one I push
into the box and let settle
as its limbs recoil in calm
resistance against the dark.

Genesis

In the beginning you knew nothing.
It was night and then day. You got up,
you went to work; you came home tired
but happy. At the end of the second
day you felt something—not discomfort
really, not pain exactly—a flux
in the chest, a ripple across the arm
like static electricity, the mind's
pinch test of alarms, among many,
it jettisons to the body. Maybe
the trees had turned just slightly,
less greenish, or shadows
lengthened, thinning to liquid darkness
on the trail; or the waxwings gathered
in their usual fluster but then settled,
unmoving, outside the deck's railing.

Interesting how I hate the midpoint
of anything, that I can tell nine-
thirty by the slant of sunlight
outside the window, how it divides
the giant maple from night to day
and back again and paints between
each branch the most painful
shade of blue. How masterful I'd
become at my own undoing, even
while you were dying, thinking *no*

no to the timing, the bruises spreading
along your back, the spark in your green
eyes failing like a ship's flare flickering
in the distance too far from shore;

day three you denied
the heaviness, the sordid
outbuildings that needed tended to,
the hunting—no energy to match
your verve—your brothers lumbering
about concerned, suspender bound,

cork boots, cans of chew.
On the fourth day there was
nothing, like the smoldering silence
before a storm, before God
called forth any kind of hope
that would get you out of bed
then send you back with headaches
and stomach pains, fatigue long past
exhaustion, a kind of deadness in the
bowels that fills the bones and loiters
in the hollows of the spine, wheedling
and afloat like dogwood blossoms
tossed into the current or trees inflamed
with sap they can't cry out. Each new

ache carried you weightless into
the fifth day to the several
slivered moons of medication,
the numbing, almost blissful
music of the drip, the chemo
pump; *such a long shot*, the

doctors warned, *from anywhere.*

And then they began, the tumors,
to birth from the spoon of sudden
wishes, lukewarm prayers; flowers
from the other side of the world
piled in but the coyote in your throat
sang its own sad diction, aware it was
being watched inside the final fix
of crosshairs. That was the sixth

day, the day we wrung our hands
and sobbed into our phones
while God declared day seven
the end of everything, the number
of completion. Your last day here
He rested in the whispers and
nods of nurses, their coming in
and going out, their clipboard
verses that could contain healing.
But in their scribblings nothing
was revealed, and God hid
in the cool of the evening
among the carolers going door
to door, in the newly strung lights
across the corridors, now sterile,
now white and void of form,
in the music floating over you and
the priests clad in purple cloth
and cardboard collars welcoming
your last *Amens.*

Salvation at 7 a.m.

I cried when my daughter told me
      how my son in law had saved
a boy's life—the kid standing randomly

outside their house, punching
      numbers into his phone, half frozen
from wandering all night stoned

or high on meth. It was January 1st,
      no way to start the New
Year with your feet stuffed into

sneakers, no socks or laces
      while the neighborhood waned
in the pre-dawn cold

long past *happy hour*, their
      friends gone home at 2
a.m. to sleep off highballs, whiskey

sours, wine stocked in basement
      bars where women in black
leggings and freshly gotten

Botox compared experiences
      at Mexican spas and prices
at the Gap. How

the sidewalk scene ruined me for days;
      my mind sweeping back
to connect the boy

with a family he believed lived
      in the vicinity, wandering
back and forth knocking

on doors that locked against
        his cries and drove temps
further down past freezing. My

son in law, a goliath of a man
        mapped in ink, his head
enshrined in self-inflicted

baldness unbolted the door
        as the boy reached
the landing's topmost step.

                        ***

My grandsons in the living room
        knee deep in Legos watch
 their father gather gloves

and sweatshirts and hurl them
        toward the boy who catches them
the way a receiver spoons a football

to his sternum and steps back onto
        the field. Once inside the truck,
the two exchange glances like strangers

struck by silence in an elevator. My Son
        in law now guesses the boy to be
somewhere in his early 20s, not a kid who'd

wear a Gold's Gym sweatshirt unsolicited
        or expect to die in it with his arms
folded across his chest, collapsed against the door.

                        ***

I go back and back as my son in law delivers him
        to an address several miles north
from where he'd walked, steers him toward

the door or waits for him to enter
        shakily into a house that appears,
itself, to be on crack; the boy, having removed

his shoes now ripe with blood, his
        toes bludgeoned with frostbite
still fumbling with his phone

were, among few others, the first
        lucid moments he considers
dumbly were his scrape with death; I

never asked but can imagine from
        my own inability to solicit
small talk or even, honestly, to resurrect

relationships, that whatever words
        had passed between them
were the broken crystals air

becomes at 12 below, and just as
        painful with the boy's feet
pressed up against the truck's dash,

the heater spewing warmth he wished
        were the fire pit of friends
he'd left that night some other life

ago and not the neighborhood
        of rabbit holes and lost
hatters he's tried desperately to leave

for the ones built with baseball
        diamonds and porches encased
in columns, their spiraling tiers of hollyhocks

and foyers of incense burners spiced with
        cinnamon and lemon feeling overmuch,
so out of reach, so much like home.

Cautionary Tales

I don't believe
what anyone tells me
about death, how you
grieve and then you
don't. I believe
in quantum physics,
and how the substance
of things retains memory,
even wood and chalk
and how, in the end,
you knew instinctively
your heart drained out
like run-off, like a thousand
rains pounding down
from the switchbacks
overhead. Or maybe
it was the world
overhead, a world
where deer loiter in a
Christmas card kind
of grace, lofty
and whole, and expectantly
quiet far above reality
where the hunted ones
go about snorting
and twitching their ears
precisely as they do
in the cautionary tales
of their kind, alarmed
by coyotes gnawing
the remaining deadness
from the ribs of a moose.
Last spring I caught
you in the kitchen not
long after the dreaded
diagnosis. You were hopeful,

though, eating whatever was
fixed for you, mowing
the lawn, shuffling around
on the land, explaining
the art of dragging
your cabins in
on chains and planting
them precisely so; and here's
where the tale gets tricky
in the undertow of all
our sorrows like the many
unanswered rivers
the future holds
before your life stopped
in that half ton place
you found yourself afloat in,
heavier than the drowned,
your body straining against
its own design to create a
protective shell something like
the bomb shelters you swore
were unavoidable, aware
the world could end abruptly
the way the world always does
despite what the forecasts say,
despite the horded cans of venison
and peeled, white potatoes.
So your body created a space
large enough to house
your spirit, but your spirit
was like smoke winnowing
in the tinder of a freshly
crafted fire and here's the deal
my friend, my brother,
it longed to bust out
like a disgruntled tenant
fed up with the rising
cost of rent; and the tale
goes it was all a kind

of nautical dusk in the
earliest stages of gloaming,
that, even hidden,
everyone sought to describe
as that despicable cliche
of *courageous attempts*
to piece yourself together,
silence your body's tremors
and scratch the restless dry
spots, imaginary or not
brought on by pills
and hallucinations,
and freight away the
plastic containers
brimming with shit
and bile. It's a tale—
twisted as your body's
cells; how they
soldiered on, those killers,
while you slept,
rifling through your
system and ghosting
away each organ,
stomach, liver,
kidneys; one by one
we filed through
your kitchen,
all of us clotted together
like avenging phagocytes
paying our last respects
to your former self,
examining the younger,
rounder you in rows of
photographs as though
you were a stranger
we'd just now met.

Isaiah 38 for the 21st Century

During a conversation with my brother, sick and despairing from Chemo treatments,I attempt to comfort him by removing God from the religious structures of our childhood—from the stained glass and churchy clichés that I believe diminish him—and instead, draw on biblical example to put God in touch, personally, with human suffering.

It was the name, *Hezekiah*, that first drew my ear to Isaiah 38. It was a name that the tongue broke off in anguish, as it spoke, and then released in awe. Still, it was the obligatory illness, which sounded less like a fairytale than the spent force of a curse—more like our grandfather, who though far from unbelieving, was spirited away in an ambulance somewhere between two counties. Because I was in bed at 3 a.m. in another town, I could only imagine his heart winding down like an old outboard in its final ebb. It took years to pen the various versions of his death, including a stint with oxygen tubes, his lips clenched, then dry and papery, fluttering as he breathed, like two birds on the edge of a storm waiting for their release. Similarly, I was linked to Charleston Heston, as supernaturally as one could get through a black and white version of The Ten Commandments, and subsequently, on the same crackling TV screen, to Kirk Douglas, who played Pharaoh. I mixed metaphors and confused parables, and all the history in-between, because I was taught to contain God in the onionskin pages of a bible whose cover gleamed from our kitchen table. Holy and untouchable. The God of this and the God of that. The God who was and not is. But what of the *revelation* I stumble upon? *I shall go softly all my years in the bitterness of my soul.* I think, now, of the bitterness of my soul, how some 4,000 years later, despite my Church-going upbringing, I'd clung dimly to life on a daily basis wishing, wanting, hoping. Not always believing in anything more powerful than the momentum of days: Getting up to go to work as swallows exploded downward from their cleft in the attic and yesterday's newspapers spoiled in the rain and defecation. I returned home to eat and sleep. Nothing I dreamed about made sense. And yet God spoke to a man who cried, who *turned his face toward the wall.* Like an old Heston film in slow motion after a tragedy has been staged, and the producers roll the scene in front of you again and again. I see him, this Hezekiah, *sick unto death*, with bed sores and crooked hands turning toward the wall, all hope stifled by the message he received: *For thou shalt die and not live.* How unfortunate to have read this as though the words were chimed by some patriarch, spewing King James verbiage, when the language was fraught with misery in the most ancient Hebraic tongue. Hezekiah could have scoffed, cursed the prophetic Isaiah to dust. With his knees curled up to his chest—in a position we've all assumed when wracked by a stomach ache or flu—in that place on the bed where it grows hot from the body's thrashing between desire and pain, he cried out to God. The bible says he *prayed.* And how. I am amazed at the defenseless yet powerful human-ness of this act. How all these years the over spiritualized teachings of the *miraculous* left me craving, not a visitation, but Kool-Aide and graham crackers in the middle of catechism. Whose fault was this? A God worse than unjust was a God who was distant, slapping our wrists, calling down pestilence on the likes of Kirk Douglas. Despite this, Hezekiah, sentenced to death, *wept sore* says Isaiah 38:3. Wept. Sore. I wept sore in the hour I saw my son, pulled from a car wreck, his eyes swelled shut. His clothes cut off of him in the hospital bed. His blood and belongings strewn over three back yards. I know Hezekiah's story, first reverently, guardedly, like all Sunday school versions delivered in a room off the sanctuary, revelation resting on the whims of whomever—usually a woman with a penchant for control—volunteered to teach. For those who mistook hobby for destiny, or more precisely for *ministry*, who blended parable with fable, there brewed a dangerous storm of unbelief, a religious Russian Roulette for each young soul. But finally it was my daughter, drunk on Vodka, who drove home the point, all piety aside, cursing and vomiting until her body lay limp on the living room floor, her knees drawn up to her chest. Sad, this view of God splattered on brick across the city, His name expressed most strongly in profanity, and at the very best, spoken of as though He was but was not to be believed as Hezekiah believed and was saved out of his sickness. I have heard thy prayer, *I have seen thy tears*...but because the tabletop bible sealed in gold could not be touched I later marked my personal bible with blotchy ink and all manner of correspondence that could easily be interpreted by a person too sick to weep. I, too, prayed, and was answered, not audibly and not by turning my face toward the wall, but by seeing our grandfather's lips unclenched and my children, meeting their appointments with death, delivered into the lives they live now.

ii: Songs of Deliverance

Fire & Water

"We say hello a thousand times and
never fully mean it. Or goodbye."
                                    —Charles Atkinson

Request

I dig through the slough

of wind burned feathers,
fish carrion swept inland

on the claws of so many birds.
I'm sitting in a pawed out

circle, fire rising
in what my hands have made

from dragging in the wrangled
tinder of falling trees.

God, I am alone,
an imagined Norseman

or a small universe
of beach pulp churning in

what is always some unsavory
relic tossed from the ocean's belly

or I'm this one thing only,
a tiny bitter scorpion muscling

my spent cargo, naked scraps
of dreams I can barely

bow to in my sleep.
Keep me alive this spring

is all I ask of you water
in the risen arc of all those

horizons already spoken for,
the ones I cannot name.

White Horse

If I never see you again, you said;
your voice, soft in the aquatic hum
of machines and tubes, trailed off
to our childhood sand box,

to us kids in the backyard;
but even as your mind soldiered
back to retrieve this thought
mine had already left for the coast—

four of us stuffed in the backseat
of our green station wagon,
heading west toward the land
of sea nekton washed

in the perigean tide and the raw
salt-ebb of sand scrubbed
to a smooth sheen, toward
sun scorched hermit crabs

swabbed to delicate crisps
under clear plastic cases we
purchased in the tourist's shops
and whose legs fell off before

we left. Waiting for your next
breath, my mind makes a jump
to the white horse arriving in the
clouds, which according to our sister,

was whipped and driven by Thor,
the god of thunder, from the land
of salps and seamounts; *how*
we feared both Thor and his horse

and ran to the house when the first claps
opened up above the sandbox, remember
that? I said, not reminding you
how the sand leaked out eventually

and its wooden frames bent toward
one another like people unable
to touch. And I could feel underfoot
the sodden sadness of late October,

snow whispering to the eaves, the ghost
of long winters rattling in the air
and the year already clearing you
from its calendar. But you

would return to the land, half there,
to the window of angels swinging
from silver cords, visitors and voices
and photographs strung together in

the bad reception seeping from the small
TV. How foreign you became to us
finally, as your son , my nephew, lifted you
from the bed; to him—a sturdy twenty

something in a CrossFit tee—you felt
like nothing, the weight of an ear bone
or an opossum shrimp caught in the
ocean's upwelling. To explain it now

I would tell you how the
sand in Oregon is not as warm
as the sand in California, nor
when we gather here on the beach

with our boxed wine and broken
hearts is the white horse thundering
above the clouds or even across the shore,
that the sky is clear and opens up

over a sandbox large enough to engulf
the world, the present and the past,
all of it tangled together like
sea kelp fresh from its strands,

from holdfasts anchoring it to the
earth where your voice is still heard
in the aquatic hum everlasting, soft
and viable in this kingdom of air
and salt.

Cannon Beach

Down from the rocks where we stowed
our dry clothing and money for the small cafe
we'd climb to afterward in the rain, we drank the mist
and scuffed the inching silt onto the shoreline.
Shell by broken shell, we pieced together a conversation
that for years had been derailed in the silent back seats
of family trips: The ones planned with good intentions,
the overstuffed bags waiting in hotel lobbies, lugged grudgingly
upstairs and eventually back down—in that ticking time bomb
of a life between parent and adolescent—were re-packed
with slightly less ferocity, less joy. From the cold Pacific
where a thousand souls before us gouged their names
into the sand, dug holes, made love, we drew a line
between our battles and dared each one to cross.
                              In twenty years it will have mattered
what we said, what detours brought us back to those rocky inlets,
the ocean's constant wash of tourists heading south to kayak, the skim
boards of our youngest two cutting shark fins through the sprays. Hour after
hour, the same braided turn of wind, bright cap, voices clapping against the
fronts that once stalled ships and added mystery to the churning sea froth in
its stew of nets. Our own sorrows, banked in that dark debris, and
trapped inside the un-tolled bells and empty boathouses of our
imaginations became the lullabies of gulls, even doves that mourned below
the coves, the clefts, the hidden places we fantasized lived Entities
far above us praying, too, for familial peace. Finally when our voices,
muffled in the swell off Haystack Rock, called out to one another,
it was to hear each others' names, and in the end, to resurrect a sign,
like a ship's white flag, that we would walk again from this bitter life
into the sweet salt air of that far-off beach.

Wildland

When the fires of 2012 swept
over 10,000 acres through
Rumsey Gulch and the Lolo Creek
Complex, you were not yet 53,
not planning to die, your body
sturdy like the type 6 engine,
quick attack truck you navigated
through thick smoke that bruised
your skin and burned the sky
to ash. Those years we believed
that life was work, all of it
to be heaved away like stones
we muscled from the ground
as kids, afterward digging post
holes in the wet soil as though
to mark our labor and return
this half century later to the
memorial of our fences strung
like broken telephone wire across
the same dark fields. How could
you know, bent over the heavy
smell of dusk falling in around us,
that one day women would bring
you gifts of food and water
in gratitude for the rescue of their
homes, the locust-like escape
of dogs and cattle, even snakes
in the porches' underpinnings
and whole garages lit like lanterns.
What was it we couldn't say? How life
burns holes in us, how even at
its best, it wrings our souls out
like those fires' wind-sped pods—
the wax currants and woodland stars,

their tiny lights gone out for acres
in the aftermath, you on initial
attack and mop up crews
freighting back between blazes in your
Nomex pants and goggles? They
say it's not the trajectory of jumpers
from their fixed wing aircrafts, their
miscalculations on exit, but those
caught in the burnovers without
emergency shelters that pose the
greatest risk, those outrun by the fire's
false weather created by intense heat
and sparks jettisoned by real wind.
It's always when we look back
that the fire overtakes us, when
our bodies push our wills beyond
containment, but even then I'd
say well done good and faithful
servant if I were your God and not
someone caught in the earth's
backdrafts spinning, spinning back
your stories from these broken fences.

Susan Doble Kaluza grew up on a cattle ranch in Northwestern Montana; she began writing poems at age 12 and publishing in small literary magazines as a college freshman under the direction of then University of Montana Director of Creative Writing, Richard Hugo. During a competitive running career which spanned over 30 years, and a short stint in summer biathlon where she earned two national Master's titles, she has worked as a newspaper columnist and fitness trainer; and now, though still training and competing, she focuses mainly on writing. "Songs of Deliverance," her debut chapbook, was a finalist in the 2017 Concrete Wolf Chapbook Award contest. Her individual poems and essays have most recently appeared or are forthcoming in *Tammy Journal; Pure Slush Australia; RATTLE; Lost River Review, as well as anthologies, New Rivers Press, Visiting Bob (a 100 poem tribute to Bob Dylan); Good Works Project;* and *Kentucky Review.*

Kaluza lives in the mining city of Butte, Montana with her husband of 35 years, and a rescue dog named Jackie Blue. She is the mother of 3 beautiful and professionally independent children, and maintains close but long distance relationships with her two youngest who reside in Portland, Oregon, and with her horse, Aria, who enjoys long breaks of marathon eating only intermittently interrupted by loping over trails in the warmer months near the border town of Eureka.

CPSIA information can be obtained
at www.ICGtesting.com
Printed in the USA
BVHW040922011118
530756BV00008BA/58/P

9 781635 347432